MILE MARKERS

Tom Moran

ISBN: 978-81-8253-839-9

First Edition: 2022
Rs. 200/-

Cyberwit.net
HIG 45 Kaushambi Kunj, Kalindipuram
Allahabad - 211011 (U.P.) India
http://www.cyberwit.net
Tel: +(91) 9415091004
E-mail: info@cyberwit.net

Printed at Repro India Limited.

Contents

Google Maps

The corner I stood my ground,
Stony Island Avenue,
where I raced across eight lanes of traffic
to get to kindergarten.
Our house,
we played "Bounce or Fly"
on the front porch.
"Over your head is a homer!"
Alleys I found what I had for nerve,
sand forts, chalk drawings at Jeffrey Park,
sacred Avalon Theater, red velvet seats,
embroidered screen curtain;
a delicate refuge
in which I was a cowboy, pilot, or child.
I log off.

I can't smell
fresh Irish soda bread in our kitchen,
how my stomach tightens
walking through a viaduct,
the warm bakery I took harbor
on winter mornings walking to St. Felicitas,
looking for my place in this louder world.
A water bug
gliding on a still pond,
moving,
just keep moving.

Computer doesn't show
spits of cruelty
at home,
the keeping quiet,
the hiding.
Some days there weren't enough rooms to hide in.

Bequeath

Earthquake in our lives
leaves rubbles and bits.
Grandpa's painting, Polish dictionary,
Mass cards, best friend's prints.
A scratched Casio watch,
alarm set at 7:30 AM;
empty wine bottle from our first date.
The harp pieces of my soul escape from.
Rosary made with flowers
from my father's wake.

I cannot pass on wealth,
but I etch my spirit
in to these trinkets.
When I'm dust,
hold them close,
feel me within.

A Gift

My friend Mike walked in front of a train. He was fourteen. In college, I worked at a hospital in the summer. On break, I sat out front and would talk with Bob who worked in the Pharmacy.
One afternoon, I came in to work and heard that Bob had gone home the night before and with his girlfriend, took an overdose of pills. They had a suicide pact. She lived, but Bob died.
When I worked for Orkin, I was friends with a tech named John. One Friday, I told John, "Have a good weekend. I'll see you Monday." On Monday, I learned John had overdosed on heroin. A needle stuck in his arm as he sat in his car in front of his apartment.
One summer night, I was driving around with friends. We came upon a group of kids. A dirty blonde angel looked in the back seat, pulled me out of the car. Twenty minutes later, my friends were rear ended at a stoplight by a drunk driver going 40 mph in a Cadillac. My friend, Steve, was crushed against the steering wheel and died; but his girlfriend lived. The bumper, trunk, and backseat where I was sitting were pushed up to the dashboard.

People fly off the potter's
wheel as wet clay.
God molds a humble mug,
grace sustains the firing.

Snakeskin

I lose what was once sacred;
time, keys, work, names.
Discarded toys
on Christmas morning,
I learn to shed precious things.

I am sugar cane
at harvest;
stalks chopped,
fed in to a grinder's wheel.
Crushed-
pulp flows
out of chutes
in to waiting buckets.

I am a child
chasing fireflies
with a Mason jar.
Who am I
to bottle light,
call it mine.

* Night Owl

The Lord is a short order cook in an all night cafe.
Pete wears a chef's hat and white T-shirt.
He wipes extra grease on his apron.
"We doze but never close"
hangs above the register.

The Lord tells me of his regulars.
Quadriplegic young man who has a party
in his hospital room because he moved his big toe.
A girl on the west side of Chicago,
blue cockroach on her arm,
crying for her lunch.
Families who sleep in cars
because they lost their home.

I taste my soup.
The anger of being shortchanged
I carried in with me
vanishes like spit on a hot rail.

*Inspired by Hopper's painting "Night Hawks"

Random Excess Memory

I do not have a flash drive mind;
my life is not skipping stones on I-phones.
There's a web site that records
weather for each day;
precise, accurate, documented statistics.
I reminisce differently.

The Tuesday my father passed was numbing,
so chordal on our wedding day.
Once I asked my mother what was
all that stuff flying through the air.
She said, "It's dandelion fluff,
from all the times
people didn't say I love you to each other."

A selfie for a life lived;
I learned that
friends didn't die,
they just ran on ahead.

Feral Epiphany

The morning of our wedding
was crystalline blue;
the sun rose twice
when you smiled.
I told you of serving a year and half
in prison for stealing money.
The look on your face
was that of a mannequin.
You thought,
weighed what I am
to what I had to do to eat.
As steel is poured
from hot ingot into forms,
you chose to go ahead
because like steel,
you know what I'm made of.

We said I do and we have.
Sunshine was served in slices at our reception.
A stray cat wandered into the party,
curled around my leg.
Purring acceptance,
it lays in our window,
gazing at time
wasted on surviving.

Over a Roaring Dam

Hear me when I want out,
when I can't feel quiet.
Hear me from darkness,
asking for redemption.

Tell me about the Golden Rule,
about Brotherhood.
Tell me about honoring my mother and my father,
honesty as a lone policy.

Show me how my pain bleeds out,
an absolution.
Show me the EXIT,
show me where I belong.

Love me like new growth
after a prairie fire,
Love me like I am of worth.

Voice whispers,
"I'm not through with you yet."

God is fluid,
and Faith floats down
as rain on my roof.

BFF'S

I was four years old,
home on my own,
but I wasn't afraid;
there were angels in the kitchen.
I'd draw smiley faces on the TV
with my mother's eyeliner;
wrap a towel around my neck,
run through the house like Superman.
The angels laughed.

One Friday afternoon,
a man on the TV said
the President was shot.
I called my father, LU 2-2799,
asked if the Russians were "gonna get me".

Now when I'm alone,
I'm not worried.
I remember the trade I made
with the angels.
I made them laugh,
they taught me to fly.

Bayou Sunrise

Wrought iron fence melts
shadows on a red door;
a black cat awakens.

New Orleans is not so far.

View of Anthony Avenue

We lived across the street
from the Chicago Skyway;
thirty feet of cement
supported the Indiana toll road.
Traffic overhead
was a cat's constant purr.
The maple sapling
my father planted
is full and lush;
he's gone,
but the tree remains.

I didn't ring the doorbell.
Another family sits on the front porch,
daydreaming of sprouting wings
to fly above the wall of concrete.

Grounded

It's hard to tell the difference
between sparrows and the homeless.
Both live in corners
of your eyes, invisible,
existing on seed and spare change.

Uneasy, I walk past
fearing it could be me
sharing the light-bulb sun of winter.

Custodial Blues

Starfish are committing suicide.
Bacteria in the ocean
is making them devour themselves.
Coral reef is bleached
by sunblock lotion in the sea.
When oil is discovered on Mars,
who will defend that planet?
Who speaks for the stars.

Each Dawn...

I walk backwards
in the wind
to shield me
from the cold.
Walk backwards
against my poetry,
hide from raw truth.
Walk backwards
from a sunrise,
to drown
in the carpeted night.

I turn,
face my words,
walk across a field
of unwritten poems.

Moonflower

Adrift at sea,
I was saved by a green-eyed mermaid;
her name is Christine.
Trading pain
as scratch farmers
on market day,
we crack matches,
set our rivers ablaze.
There are saplings,
there are the Redwoods.
There are swimming pools,
there is the Pacific Ocean.
There are gorges,
there is the Grand Canyon.
There is Love,
there is what I feel for you.
You are a moonflower
blooming at night,
whose lilac fragrance
seeps into our bedroom window,
scents my dreams.

We are two raindrops
folded into one;
wait on the day when we'll realize
Jesus has everyone's eyes.
We are bits pulled from sourdough batter,
set aside to add to the next batch
to keep the recipe alive.

This Property is Posted

I walk my dog in to the prairie,
take him off leash.
It's late in the winter day,
my breath is balling up.
Pat takes off into the tall grass,
all that remains from the florid summer.
I catch glimpses of him leaping
in the air to nab rabbits.
My shadow wants to go home.

I call and call,
but he does not respond.
He could have gone this way or that,
but there is no snow to follow his tracks.
I look in places he hasn't gone before,
like a poet searching new forms.
Traveling in undisturbed grass,
I'm a trespasser of poems.

....Has Been Disconnected

My older brother taught me
to ride my bicycle.
I leaned against a pole
to develop balance;
once mastered,
I rode where I had to go.
I haven't known him in years.
He lost his balance,
fell off-
and I have no poles
for him to lean on.

Slivers

*Sleep is the gift of many spiders,
memories stick to their web.
I see you friend;
silently, I awake to your absence.
Dreams cling to my morning,
making me weep.

Life is a thin line between two eternities;
what you were before you were born,
what you'll be after you're gone.

*First line from a Carl Sandburg poem

Heirlooms (A one sided conversation at my Father's grave)

I'm now the age
my Father was
when he gave me my last beating.
I told him
if he touched me again,
"I'll kill you."

I wish his anger bled
as easily as his knuckles.
Is there a part of me like that?
I leave bruises
at his grave
as flowers.

Meditations on Light

I cup a firefly
in my hand,
marvel at its
self-generating luminesce.
I let it fly
to join dozens of
other fireflies.
Together, they look like
an army camp burning
fires before a battle;
or maybe all the times
I knew
you won't be here
in the morning.

A Tenant of the Current

I play my harp,
birds tweet in key.
River slices deeper,
notes go lower.
I'm being pulled in.

Music is a river;
I must learn the difference
between thirst and drowning.

Too Cold for Words

Ideas are frozen as fish in a pond.
I have desire
but wait on guidance.
A poem of loss, excess,
or perhaps the past.
I know now though, the past
is asbestos;
if you don't disturb it,
it can't hurt you.

As a child, I threw a blanket
over a clothesline,
anchored it with clothespins.
I would open the flap a crack
and snap it shut
if anyone peeked in.
Such is poetry.

Red cardinal splotches on the colorless snow;
trees silently dream of green leaves
to hide their spartan frame.
God scrapes scales of fish
that drift down like snow.

Perennial Blues

Good
kids are
pruned before
they can blossom.
Their deaths leave bare spots
in a tender garden.
A silent play lot;
I cry inside
for a bud
that won't
bloom.

9/12/2001

Sun slides up.
I wake to vacant skies;
only the sound of birds at work.
I reach down
to pick up the newspaper.
Headlines say,
"America is Wounded."
Front page photos show
loved ones threading New York streets
searching for survivors.

I whisper,
"The world will not end this way,
it will not end this way."

Lincoln's Blues

It's the first time
I'm in your house.
I brought the flowers
from your wake.
You lived on Wilson Street,
north of the Burlington tracks.
The arrangements look like a lily jury.
Crows pick at shiny things.

You moved to Illinois
to be a parent.
Next door lived Mr. Walters,
who "was born a week before Moses."
Millie and Billie lived across the street.
Billie played Willie Nelson at night.
One day, Billie's new pick-up truck was stolen.
Crows pick at shiny things.

You lived four houses
from Mrs. Zimmer;
her son enlisted in the Army.
She once showed you his medals.
He's now three rows over from you.
Mrs. Zimmer's son won't be re-upping.
Crows pick at shiny things.

You had to join
a local religion.
No one was there of your faith.

The church is west of town,
near Adams and Main,
on a hill,
where you said, "they feel closer to God."
Crows pick at shiny things.

I have more flowers to deliver.
The owner of the combination
funeral parlor, ambulance service, and furniture store,
said she would leave the east drive door open.
I load my van with your cargo.
The lady says her family's been in business
over a hundred years.
Crows pick at shiny things.
You were waked a week after
the Williams boy. He lived with his aunt.
You said he was a good kid,
but after another fight, the police were called.
Cops *said* he had a knife.
You said they didn't give him a chance.
It was "pure murder."
Crows pick at shiny things.

You worked at the chemical plant.
That's where you said you got the cancer that killed you cousin.
Two other people have died working there.
But you needed the money and liked the life;
the plant is still killing people,
but nobody cares.
There are no regrets from board meetings.
Crows pick at shiny things.

You have all the flowers now.
They'll comfort you for a time,
but will wither and subside.
I head back home on the road north.
You belong to the stars and memory now,
your casket lowered home.
The handles sparkle with the bronze sun.
Crows pick at shiny things.

Just 'tis

I help my mother
down the stairs;
same hands I once held
crossing greedy streets
stocked with hungry cars
that ate little children.
Same hands
that pinned a note
on my shirt,
"Please sell Tom a pack of Newports."
I'm resigned to the reality
she won't live forever.

We conquer the stairs,
thank each other with silence.
What is broken
can meld together;
there must be love,
there *must* be forgiveness.

Looking Out the Back Door of Jackie B's Laundromat

Metra train pulls into
the station and
commuters leak out.

Raising painted umbrellas,
they drift across the ponding parking lot
like Monet's water lilies,
scattering in different directions.

I soak up the stillness,
wait for my dollars' worth of
drying time to end.

How Long Has it Been

I crawl in to your sweet eyes,
curl up,
like a beat dog.
I sleep in your sighs,
journey in to your night.
I awaken,
breathing the light of a new day.
You are the precious
life of morning.
I love you.

Goodbye

When you walk in the country
she further confided to me,
you may chance to meet with
substantial shadows on your road.
Life is a race with nightmares.

The dawn is gray here,
she went on to tell me.
It was always like this.
We don't know whom to accuse.
I want what I paid for!

I add one further word to you,
a question rather-
Does water flow in your prayers too?
Hospice is a train station.

I am writing to you from the end of the world,
you must realize this.
Trees often tremble.
There is no choir.

www.ingramcontent.com/pod-product-compliance
Lightning Source LLC
Chambersburg PA
CBHW022204160726
48282CB00024B/321
9788182538399